a sweeter song

a sweeter song

Catharsis

DR. MARTINA McGOWAN

Illustrated by DIANA EJAITA

Published by Sourcebooks
P.O. Box 4410, Naperville, Illinois 60567–4410
(630) 961-3900
sourcebooks.com

Library of Congress Cataloging-in-Publication Data

Names: McGowan, Martina, author.
Title: A sweeter song : catharsis / Dr. Martina McGowan.
Description: Naperville, Illinois : Sourcebooks, 2024. | Includes bibliographical references.
| Summary: "A Sweeter Song moves beyond the rage of McGowan's first poetry collection
by showing that there is more than one dimension to the lives of people of color, women,
and other marginalized and oppressed peoples, focusing on universal issues we all face as
human beings. The issues covered in this collection include, but are not limited to: Personal
history/ Parents/ Ancestors Love/Lust/ Loss Biblical Religion Death/Dying/ Aging War /
Politics"-- Provided by publisher.
Identifiers: LCCN 2023028445 (print) | LCCN 2023028446 (ebook) | (trade paperback)
| (epub) | (pdf)
Subjects: LCGFT: Poetry.
Classification: LCC PS3613.C49425 S94 2024 (print) | LCC PS3613.C49425 (ebook) |
DDC 811/.6--dc23/eng/20230626
LC record available at https://lccn.loc.gov/2023028445
LC ebook record available at https://lccn.loc.gov/2023028446

Printed and bound in the United States of America.
VP 10 9 8 7 6 5 4 3 2 1

I dedicate this book to my amazing daughter, Amanda. Thank you for reading early drafts and giving feedback, for listening to readings, and for being one of my most important life teachers.

I also dedicate this book to my mother, Sarah, and my father, Walter.

Sameron adion aso

I shall sing a sweeter song tomorrow.

Contents

I

Mother's Day Aubade	1
A Song for My Mother, The Missing Sestina	3
The Abettor Speaks	5
On the Subject of Mothering	7
The Kindness of Strangers	8
Delivery: Just outside the door	11
Sankofa (Home: Who We're From)	14
Love Recast in Fire	17
Lost Song	18
Flying Lesson	20
Translation	21
The Blue Room	24
Lilies of the Valley	26
Cartography	27
Croton	29
A Sweeter Song	31

II

Once I Thought I'd Found True Love (A Villanelle)	35
Nothing More to Say	37

What If We Were Brave   39

Lost in Time   41

Easy to Love   44

Hypnopompic Stirrings   46

Waking Alone   47

Love Like Poetry   49

After (the Rain)   50

The Nonsynoptic Gospels   52

Heart Math   53

Time to Go   54

III

Death   59

Seventy (A Sonnet)   60

A Blessing for My Future Self   61

Hands   62

Coronach   64

Cornelian Glimmer   66

Titanic   68

Full Spectrum   70

What Remains   72

The End (A Sonnet)   75

Promise   76

Scomparsa   77

IV

How to Destroy the World	81
Fossicking	83
Predictive Crises	84
A Litany of Fear and Loss (A Cento)	86
The Fullest Life	89
Echolalia	91
Happy Juneteenth	92
Americans Won't Wear THAT Mask	95
Lingers	97
Babylon	99
Once the Fog Has Lifted/Pandemic Pause	101
Dual Citizenship	105
Once Dipped: Emergence	107
Articulations	109
Revelations from a Riot	110
Epode to Tedium (Are We Post-Pandemic Yet?)	112
Why I Can't Watch the News	114
Waiting	116
Each Other's Business	117
America, the Repugnant Republic (A Golden Shovel)	119
Sobriquets	121
Video Prevarication	123
Prey	127

Birthing Dead Boys   129

Ode to a Failed Coup   131

Smoking Gun   134

Treadmill of Hate   136

We Rise   137

Not Lost   138

When Archeologists Speak   140

The Muses of Wartime   142

Invisible Tribes   145

Wellness Check   146

V

The Hum   151

Letting Go   153

Ode à Laranja (Ode to the Orange)   155

The Sea Goddess Calls   158

The Dunes at Twilight   160

Winter Is Coming #70   162

The Little Death   164

Chasing Joy   166

Becoming Ourselves   168

Single Socks in Absentia   169

Ode to Dawn   170

A Sonnet to Morning's Door   172

Hope is…(A Sonnet)   173

Alchemy   174

Fear of the Edge   175

Scriptor Poetica   177

Sentimental Trees   178

Ode to An Underrated Food   179

Gossamer Dreams   180

The True Cost   181

Catharsis   182

VI

Elegy for Eve   187

No Angels Came to Save Us   188

Crafting Beyond the Half-Century Mark   191

Advice to a Crafter   193

Earth Mother (An Ekphrastic)   195

J'Accuse (An Ekphrastic)   197

Borderless and Boundless   199

VII: Acknowledgments

Acknowledgments: The Work   203

Acknowledgments: The People   205

Mother's Day Aubade

The iron scent of afterbirth.
As I rise
to the temptation of gazing
into your shining face one more time.

Through a maze of rooms
where they seek
to temper your light.

They unwrap
The swaddling you now wear
Instead of the cheery onesie in my bag.

Product of love
Of a now empty womb. Too soon, too late.
Premature benediction.

Here you are, cool to my touch.
All but emptied of warmth we once shared.
Almost beyond my reach.

What shall I dream for you now, my love?

I wish you wings
to fly beyond this place and time.

I wish you seraphim
clanging cymbals at your rising!

A brightly burning sun
to light your daytime path.
Starlight as nightlight.

Muhammadan angels strumming pipas,
singing plain chant lullabies.

Free range throughout the cosmos
Astride your unicorned mare.
I. Wish. You. Here.

A Song for My Mother, The Missing Sestina

I often write about my father,
Never enough about my mother.
The poems I do not write are not light.
It was not cheery, by anyone's measure.
No untroubled frolic through childhood, mine.
But neither only desolate nor darkness.

As children we are often in the dark
about the union of our folks. Further
along we're able to explore, to scrutinize
The love that must have blossomed, our mothers,
Younger, considered the full measure
Of our fathers, before stepping united into life's light.

Grandfather, a freed slave, baptized, enlightened.
Only to find a world still full of darkness.
Migrating north, seeking a different measure
Of the value of our skin. Broken father.
An untimely demise. Forsaken mother.
Left with a teen, thought she'd lost her own damned mind!

The poems I do not write might help underline
The dark days, the loss of her joy, the loss of her own light.
They would speak of courageous choices. My mom
Struggling to save her girl-child from the dark.
Moving our legacy to some degree further.
Raising the bar with fresh standards, new measures.

Love cannot always be calculated or measured
While hurt is still assailing our hearts and minds.
She made the leanest of wages stretch further and farther.
Praying one day the burden might lighten.
Generational curses lurking in the dark.
Boldness in things betokening a good mother.

The poems I do not write for my mother
Would talk about a love I now treasure.
For in our youth, useful gauges can't be found in the dark.
Squirming through troubles and sidestepping landmines.
Slowly limping toward the ardent light.
Both silently grieving, missing my father.

The darkness did not devour my mother.
And by any appraisal, she was a creator.
Lessons I share with mine, to keep searching for life's bright light.

The Abettor Speaks

Grown from mean streets,
I am the uninvited child:

Hard-drinking, chain-smoking fiend,
friend. Freak looking for the next fix—

Flawed by my own jealousy, avarice,
Racing, rushing toward my own demise.

The twin who's never felt warmth.
Tricked, driven, silenced, buried.

The assassin, just out of sight.
Folding the dark around us like a cloak.

A matryoshka. Living inside the boy
who loves, inside the girl who cannot,

Inside the boy missing his father
Inside… Always inside.

The child caught beneath pulsing manhood.
The part that never rose from that bed

Of affliction. The leftover piece.
Abused destined to become abuser.

A collage, held together by thin wire.
Keeping the schizophrenic break at bay.

A genetic patchwork of hate.
The ruse de guerre.

I am family—mother / father, wife /
sister, brother / husband. A self-contained narrative.

The hidden self, the darker kin.
The remainder seeking to be made whole.

I am our sin eater for all our wickedness.
Sitting in our hidey-hole

I am death.

And I am waiting.

On the Subject of Mothering

After Mila Haugová

I cannot tell you anything about that
Unsure as I am of my own proficiency.
But, one day, for a few moments, the world will be quiet.
Then, suddenly, like Eve, seeing her son the first time
You can name another.

Your heart will swell with joy and pride
And settle into a comfortable peace
Knowing part of you now resides elsewhere
Seeing yourself through compelling eyes
Watching yourself in actions and thoughts

And then, my precious heart,
you will both know love
And no matter how fleeting, feel its power.
And begin to find your way forward
To a place no one can ever explain.

The Kindness of Strangers

When I was about 3 feet tall
An acquaintance of my mother
Presented me with a red, plastic umbrella
Decorated with white polka-dots

It was marvelous and slick
And cool to the touch

A place to take refuge
When the world was raining down
On my personal parade both
Physically and metaphorically

I carried it everywhere
Until the metal began to bend at awkward angles
And the plastic tore beyond repair

When I was about a foot taller
We met again
I remembered her face and her kindness
And her name

More importantly, I remembered
The simple, loving gesture
To a quiet, lonely child
Of a gift, costly to her, I'm sure
And dear to me

I still appreciate her
For seeing me
When no one else could or did
And for the enduring lessons of showing kindness

Even when we don't feel there's much to share
There is always something to give
And every act is important

Taller still, and many years older
Working in a hut-hospital in Haiti
From an exam room hotter that Hell
Propping the only window open for a breeze

I spied 3 little girls playing out back
They are about 3 feet tall
Probably small for their age
I could see they didn't have much

Clandestinely, I passed them the day's ration

Nutrition bars and a sandwich

Delighted giggles and Mercis follow

Perhaps one day when they are taller

they too will remember kindness

And pass it on

Delivery: Just outside the door

The soon-to-be-dad has chosen to pace and wait
Just outside the door
Until summoned

His wife and I enter
A dance we've been practicing
For nearly a year

Minds in synch. Face-to-face, skin-to-skin.
We turn
    we sway
        we rock
            we chant
                we laugh
                    we sweat
                holding hands
            we embrace the pain, together
    We count
We push. Yes, even me.

I see a bit of hair
She leans into the nurse
I lean into her
"We have ears!"
Above the mask, she reads my smiling eyes
She smiles back at me

We take a pause
Breath normally for just a beat
Then return to battle stations
Push!   Push!
One last time.   Push!

I fold the new life into my arms
Clearing its mouth
And examine it quickly

Silently reciting my blessing
"Welcome to one of the best days of your life.
This day you are the center of the universe.
And you are loved by everyone."

Cord already clamped.

Clandestinely, I now cut it.

Passing the bleary-eyed infant to meet its mother,

 face-to-face for the first time.

 Hearing her voice clearly,

 undampened by the waters of life

Blessing them both a final time

Inviting the father to join us from just beyond the door

I set to work

Keeping watchful eyes on the mother, child, and father

They sometimes faint

I assess the damage, the blood.

My hands transitioning to their natural cadence

Of repair.

I thank the universe.

For I am the captain and the chaplain of this ship

And today we have all arrived at port safely

And swaddled in love.

Sankofa (Home: Who We're From)

Plucked from starlight, playing in forests.
Passing through the Gates of Hell and barracoons.
13 days inside the belly of another beast.
Highland heather lashed to my DNA.

Up from the sticky, sweet sap of stout pines.
Barbed and prickly cotton, 200 pounds a day
Flesh, timber, fluffy bolls all for auction block.
Tumbled-down slave quarters turned to homes.

From emancipated slaves bearing biblical names.
Grandmothers dreaming of Freedom with a capital F
Cotton-scarred hands corralling the future.
Sharing history not found in books.

We are from red clay pounded into concrete.
Hard streets and harder women
Doling out wisdom and hard-earned lessons.
Love buried deep, like diamonds, hard to see.
Sometimes harder to feel.

From running across hot, tarry rooftops
Wise potato chips and orange Nehis.
Marbles, stickball, and flying free from swings,
Before we knew we were prey.
Again.

Tiny apartments, filled with family,
Aromas of foods from down home.
A blessed circle big enough for "Jesus wept!"
To be said more than once.

Smiling eyes cutting, side-rolling, waiting
For another to say, "He sure did!"
Risking a finger-pluck from one aunt
And the death stare from another.

Fathers who adored us, but drank too much,
Crushed beneath the world's weight. Brothers
who loved too many. Others molesting
those they could not love. Women, besting the evil tide.

From people, who learned beating as remedy and correction
Pushing their children's hearts away. Hoping
to save them from corruption, from death.

Rising.
Continuing to imagine
Worlds better than we received.

This is a song woven through many generations
holding one long breath.
Sharing the story.
So that other can see that hope thrives inside our pain
And that home lives on inside our hearts.

Love Recast in Fire

The absurdities of our youthful lives
Untidy trammels to maturation
Somehow, miraculously survived

Spontaneous combustion sets alight the clothing
On the back of our bedroom door
Somehow my fault—or maybe not

Nonetheless, a hasty prayer sent forth
What do I have to trade
For my grandmother's life?

How many oaths and promises
Can be sworn in 30 seconds?
How many memories can be processed
With a blazing inferno before your eyes?

The substance and endurance of love
Recast, reforged, reimagined
Breaks us wide open, like newborn babes
In the face of fear, flames, and forfeiture

Lost Song

In the beginning there was sound. Muted.
Perhaps a melody hummed to us in the void.

A word. Becomes a line, becomes a song.
The rhythm lost at birth.

Circles of love build and release.
We love and let go. Love and let go.

Spirit bruised many times.
Betrayed by life. Betrayed by death.

Mended but changed.
Forward, backward, we weave our way

Until we meet ourselves once again.
And maybe that is how it ends.

The original song finally remembered.
Perhaps as a poem this time.

The ensō closes.

Life. Complete.

Flying Lesson

Two dimes appear, like magic,
From pendulous breasts
Placed into my sweaty, summer palm
For dreaming a lucky number.

Off, up the hill to the closest bodega,
Greedily searching the case
I cannot find what I want.

The street in front of me, a fence behind
An insignificant barrier, a 150-foot drop
Looking both ways I head down the hill

I step out. Gentle slow motion ensues
Dimes forgotten, on their own trajectory
I watch my aunt rise from her stool

I sense the moment she knows it's me
That odd duck.
The one just here.
Flying...

Translation

For my Father

One summer day
When I was small
You left for work
And never came home

When I was small
I searched for you
Never thinking you'd rest
In the red clay of home soil
So very far
From me

I talked to trees
And to leaves
Cloudless skies
The heavens
Even the walls
Of my tiny room
Hoping
You could hear me
See me

In my brokenness
In spaces
That could scarce contain my grief

Not knowing the names of constellations
In the blackness and blankness of space
I'd link several stars together
With you always as the brightest
And talk to you there
Akin to praying
But not

Now,
The full spread of wings
Of eagles or falcons
Makes me smile

You are there
Sometimes
Flying,
Racing across the sky
High
Majestic
And Royal

Sometimes you are here
Standing beside me
Guarding my heart

My heart knows
I will always find you
In the wings
Not in the heavens
So far away
From me
Not yet
If ever

As I enter
My own translation
Away from those I leave
Gloved, grounded

Perhaps
I too
Can become an eagle
Or something else
Worthy of remembrance

The Blue Room

Licenses collected; warnings issued.
There is a place on the river
Where the water is lightning fast, forceful,
Difficult to manage.
Because rivers and rocks can never be managed.
Even the Mississippi remembers.
We resign to manage ourselves.

Slow water to learn the commands.
We crest the rise
And see BFR for the first time
Coxswain shouting orders
6 neophytes oarsmen under the lash, trying to comply

Before we find our rhythm, we strike.
Taking flight
Losing my paddle
Plunging into the turbulence

Into the river surprisingly peaceful, beautiful
Eerily calm, undemanding

Half longing to stay inside the quiet
The raft floats overhead
Showering me with blue.

A few strokes and I bob to the surface.
Lots of screaming and pointing
But I cannot understand

They toss a lifeline
And I know I must return
One hand grasps the rope
And then the next
And then the next

I brought them here
I must take them home.

Lilies of the Valley

The scent of lilies always carries me back.
Their treacly perfume,
Testaments to lives well-lived
Or to lives, well, just done

Images dance across our eyes
Draw us into sweeter moments
Summoning smiles, tears, and pain
Trips down memory lane

Coupled with self-examination
Seeking truths, facing the misremembered,
Or perhaps reimagined recollections
Archived in our hearts

Homage paid to the corporeal
Releasing the spirit
Across the bonds of time and space
Until we meet again

Cartography

It was not on any map or blueprint
Not prophesied by any palmist
The heavens must have ensured that
We could get from "there" to "here"

The princess settled in your big blue Buick
Surrounded by brackish snacks
Swathed in love

You, drowning your sorrows
Mourning losses, life unfulfilled
Secrets I had yet to learn

What map could have adumbrated
What would become
Of our two damaged spirits

Because I knew you
Because I knew love
Because I lost you

I continue our lonely dance,
Moving my feet to half-remembered music
That only I can hear.

And, oh, how I miss you
Still

Croton

Running. Scrabbling over hard stones.
Heading up hills we've not yet conquered
Stumbling upon a meadow we stop to marvel at it.

Warding off contempt and mockery
Of our everyday concrete existence
Out and free, we'll not spoil the moment

With thoughts of what we do not have
Nor with desire to refashion our worlds
There is beauty to be found in each.
Picking a few flowers for our favorite adults

To fuel our arguments to stay late enough
For the fireflies to come out and dance with us
They may fall on deaf ears, but the game's
The thing. So, we will plead our case.

A cool breeze catches the scent of summer,
of sweaty skin. Wonder rekindled.

Excitedly, we run off again. Further,
Deeper into the forest of discovery.

And to hold the rest of the world at bay.
A little while longer

A Sweeter Song

After Ethridge Knight

You ask for sweeter songs
Better rhymes and lighter melodies
But my poor heart cannot comply
For the truth is all we have on offer

Promises of light-filled days, remain empty
Lasting happiness, in short supply
Islands of joy, contentment
Sinking in seas of setbacks

I too dream of fresh breezes caressing my face
Walking white sands, chasing waves
Wallowing in wildflower fields,
Toes dipping carelessly into cool creeks
Basking in moonlight, beneath a blanket of stars

Awaiting the opening of asylum doors
Cosigning my sluggish freedom
Anxious to release the sorrow, the heartache
And watch them float away

31

Some other day, I shall sing to you of peace,
and love, and hope
Some other day, I shall write of beauty and nature
But not this day…

Today, I am but a canary
Caught in life's coal mine
Inhaling double doses of air
So that *you* may breathe

II

Once I Thought I'd Found True Love
(A Villanelle)

But we ended up breaking up
Left lost, alone, betrayed, afraid
I instead found myself waking up.

Next to a boy, I thought a man, staying up
Late at night, discussing kids, me, being played,
not sensing that we were already breaking up.

A foolish heart, not yet versed in making up
lies about love. Easily taken in by every charade.
Eventually I got back on track by scraping up

Pieces of my broken pride. Seeing the difference between
    making love
And just getting fucked
Thank god we wound up breaking up!

Getting a grip and taking up
My own time. Fumbling through the shade
Cast my way. And in this time, I found myself waking up

To brighter days. Knee-deep in life's river finally facing up
To the red flags I overlooked and the part I played.

Once I thought I'd found true love. We ended up breaking up.
Instead of feeling forlorn, forsaken, I found myself.

Nothing More to Say

The falling leaves become the first
winter snow. The chill
has crept into my heart.

This is the door it always chooses. How
I know it's the beginning of arctic frost.
Disaffection has arrived.

Grief mingles with anger and sadness.
All struggling to hide below the surface.
Camouflaged, drifting just out of sight.

I'll not disparage our laughter or joys.
We needed each other for a time.
But I won't lie to myself again.

And though the end comes toward us slowly
I know this drifting cannot be mended.
I've tried before and disaster still found us.
My heart always longs for better endings.

We will be together a bit longer.

But in the end, you too will realize

I had already slipped from your grasp,

You from mine.

You simply did not perceive the moment,

And there was nothing more to say at the time.

What If We Were Brave

What if we were brave learned to sip
The undrinkable, stood steadfast
Unmovable facing our seemingly
Complicated circumstances

What if we could synchronize our feelings
To this moment perfecting pitch and rhythm
The way our hips move matching the desires
Of our feet, and hearts, and hands
When we dance, and walk, and love

What if we assume we know who or what
We want at the end of our days
Knew we would survive any
ruffling of feathers and feelings

Could we re-learn to breath so deeply
We'd calm our own racing, rebellious hearts

What if we wore memorial stones
Of lost loves and missed opportunities

As pendants, as precious to us as pearls
Would our truths then permeate our marrow
Tamping down our tendency to doubt
Keep us off the trail of self-sabotage

Would our wills and backbones stand tall
As we surrendered only to nature's truth
What if we acted bravely this one time
Together

Acknowledge that we only have loan
Of this tiny sliver of infinity
Could we weather the storms we might conjure

Or will we still stand motionless
In anticipation of further signs
From a universe that has already spoken

Let an eternity of happiness
Elude us one more time
Perhaps forever

No. Let us choose to be brave together
Risking all for ourselves for love

Lost in Time

You
Drifting in some gear I cannot align
Sometimes, changing so quickly
I struggle to follow

Sometimes,
You know who you are
Who I am
But, not always,
Not today

Searching, mining
My own memories for the name
You call me today,
That is not my own

Love demands I trace
The time and dimension
Of your current location

I try to calm

Your distress
Our distress

All too often
I cannot retrieve answers quickly enough
And I am afraid we are somehow
On the same walkabout
Into oblivion

Almost magically the gears shift
Flopping us both back into the present

This makes you sad
You know you have missed a beat
Lost your place in our dance

How I wish I could hold your hand
To pull you forward
Or backward
So we could travel the same road
More frequently

Mine some passage and find my way
Into the elastic and velcro

That now holds your mind hostage

To weave the metrics
Of time's flow
For you

But, maybe
I do not
wish to know the future too well

Perhaps
The same daemon
Stalks my path
And I will know
When the time is ripe

Or possibly
I will not
Know at all

Lost in time
Waiting for my guide to take my hand
Or just waiting...

Easy to Love

Moving with an easy grace
Inside

Dancing
Together, apart

Reaching for your hand
Automatically drifting into each other

Stepping into our private space
We look deeply into each other

And smile, and kiss
And then we laugh,

We always laugh
Like new and curious lovers.

Your smile warms me
In all the hollow and the hurt places.

Grateful to find someone to love
And I pray that I am easy to love too

Hypnopompic Stirrings

Roused by thoughts of the night's search and rescue
for truth and treasure. Nostrils filled
With your scent. Joints protesting. Timeworn
Muscles pulling against gravity.

I pull you closer, marry your flesh to mine
As if I can protect you from the world
And hold you as mine alone
A memory, a smile, a kiss to carry us through

Until we reconvene
Here
On this stage, this altar
This sanctuary
Now dedicated
To our love and to our rest

Waking Alone

Bright schemes from ethereal dreams
Emerge from long forgotten memories
As we rise from the deep

Like the tentative footsteps of toddlers, thoughts
Clamber toward the first light of day
Reignites hope, rekindles spirit

Lovers lost
Some imagined
Harry my head and heart

Now consigned to near-oblivion
and troubling dreams
Dwelling in happier places than I could have rendered
I hope

Paramours in memory's chaotic chronology
Sweet songs of youth
Somber songs of midlife
Soulful songs of age

All remind me that I am loved

That I was loved

And loved in return

As I touch the cool side of the bed

Love Like Poetry

Love like poetry
An impossible blessing
A silent mirror

Words unbidden
Spring from the muses
Prickling our senses

Loose from gravity's grip
Sending us aloft
With but an idea

After (the Rain)

Love's tempestuous thunderstorm
The earthy aroma that fills our nostrils
when love feels fresh and new
still probing,
still questioning
Still deciding
Is it safe?

Moving from gentle drops of rain
To assail us keeping pace
With the quickening of our passion
Rising and falling
Sousing us in the satiety
Of being loved and touched
And held by another

In time the storm subsides
The rain diminishes
Vanishes
Spent
Forlorn

Forsaken

Once again

But still,

We continue to sniff the atmosphere

Our spirits reminiscing

Thirsting

For petrichor

The Nonsynoptic Gospels

The nonsynoptic gospels of our lives
Discordant
For the parts we just don't get
Hoping to understand better
By and by

Often choosing parasites over men
And women who might love us better
By design. Half bent in love
Watching the moon meander
Following its downward arc
Before all is lost

Although if we had read more carefully
We would have seen
It was all irrationally predictable
By the dissonant gospels of love
And life

Heart Math

Worn like hand-me-down shoes
Scuffed, broken in, and finally
No longer pinching at the corners

Keeping us warm like a time-worn quilts
With scents of former times
Of people and days

Minds labor with the division
Of love. The multiplication of it
With no leftover duplicity.

Yet our hearts divine
The exact amounts of love we can give
Of what we have received in turn

Time to Go

For Simon Armitage

You can almost see their agents just outside your vision
You never know when the summons will arrive
You only know it will

Like tedious foreplay, this agonistic dance begins the same way
Pushing papers aside, the startled Pekingese face rises in my
    direction
Surrounded by its Brillo pad fading to grey steel

Beady, little eyes lurk
Behind the slow blink of the final curtains closing
The Grotte des Deux-Ouvertures pulls at my scent

Teeth, treacherous jetty stones
Morph into a rictus smile
And a pitiless, chilling chuckle

Stiffly rising, backside as straight as an ironing board
Teetering toward me, aspiring to normal height
Toes on display like mewling, newborn moles

Dressed in vintage conservative Barbie
Arm, the broken limbs of winter reach for my hand
Bat claws moving with the enthusiasm of a long dead fish

We sit, and speak
I listen to the lizard tongue that holds little truth
Doling out promises as dusty abandoned crypts

And every time we meet
The wolf in me can sense the hunter
Sniffing the air, looking for blood

We will not do this dance for long
I wish you well, wrapped in your misery and doubt
I must move on, or risk becoming you

Death

Stunned, yes

Then came the tears
The calm, the fears
Locums sidling into the breaches
The space holders, the heart fixers

Then came time, the years
The ceaseless ebb and flow of grief.
Growth and clarity
Accepting all mortality

Then perception, pain notwithstanding
Finally understanding
It could have happened
No other way

Acquiescing.
That all bright suns
Are borne of star clusters
Whose extinction changes everything

Seventy (A Sonnet)

We enter the final quarter.
A great mixture of beginnings and endings
Flashbacks of tenderness, love, and strife
Births, teen angst, funerals, and weddings.

Recounting the many failures and glories
Old dramas and traumas nipping at our heels
Standing as heroes of our own stories
Finally tasting simplicity sans analyses.

Grace and mercy, received and bestowed
Bodies slowed as strength and time demand
Taking pride in most of the seeds we've sowed
Prepared to share learning, lend a hand

To now wallow in fear and loss would be tragic
A new journey starts. Learning to trust in its magic.

A Blessing for My Future Self

After Lucille Clifton

Whatever the time remaining to me
Whether it is 15 minutes, 15 summers or infinity
I'll trust the legacy I leave behind
To speak in remembrance of me
Beyond this secular capacitance

May my mind continue to expand
Rightly processing, holding love secure
My eyes, seeking unanticipated joys,
Wondrous potential in everything
And in all I meet in these final days

Sailing from this to that, and farther on
Hands working appointed, anointed tasks
Sharing the stories so others can see us
Pouring light into dark and dismal spaces

Paving new roads for others. Sharing
my heart's blessings. Seeding the ground we've tread
with discernment. Finding forever peace
And tranquility as we continue.

Hands

The hands are among the first to go
First, they lose their strength, then beauty
Then one day you'd swear they were someone else's
Perhaps your grandmother's

The tiniest of scar is on my right index finger
My daughter claims she cannot see
As I share a story, a memory with her daughter

A pet adoption gone awry
Of two near feral cats from the SPCA
Proving I neither understood the cats
Nor my children well enough at the time

A single parent's attempt at cementing bonds
Losing one anyway

The gash received while re-boxing them
Driving through a Houston monsoon
A makeshift bloodied bandage around my good hand

The walk of shame as I returned them
knowing what came next

A day we learned something important
About ourselves and each other

Coronach

What a special gift if we could just kiss
Away the word "cancer," or lessen its blow.
The way some mothers can kiss away pain.

Offering frail support, watching life
wither away. Bearing witness
to lives well lived, while still living.

Invisible barbarians chipping away
at vitality. Slowly sapping strength
like water seeping from ice too warm.

Trying to pour light in where it threatens
to be extinguished, to keep brilliance alight
Shoring up hope where it has been all but defeated.

Mere onlookers, voyeurs before
the spectacles of living and dying
In our own dance toward death's door.

Facing the decaying hourglass,
Combing through the grist and grain of frail
and fading memories with a tortured heart

Tears threatening to overrun their levees
I sit to compose a final song
For you, my love.

Cornelian Glimmer

What is asked of us?
Not the monuments we build
To their postmortem estimation
Seeking to honor them, or is it ourselves?

Not the whipping of our consciences
Losing ourselves in contemplation
Of what we could have done better, different
Not a heavy-handed ersatz replication

Of their lives' successes and failures
Becoming ragged and orphaned aspirants
Cast into their mortal images.
There is nothing they need from the living.

What have we to offer? The cornelian glimmer
Of our hearts to accompany
Them to whatever comes next, casting
Them into the amber light of memory.

Shining a bright mirror on their humanity

Heeding faults and foibles

And learning from every fragment

Of who they were

As we shape and reshape

Our own destinies

Without them

Titanic

We make provisions to save everyone
But we do not know how to save ourselves

Cheers from those we think we've helped to save
Jeers from those damned by our action or inaction

Touch our spirits lightly as we press on
Riding the tidal pools of pain, trauma

Churning inside and beset from without
We cannot save ourselves

A shadow of a ghost
A vagabond, walking through this life

Witnesses, sentries, temporary
Constellations of expected endings

The left-behind will say gone too soon

But it can never be too soon

We can only go at the right time

For we were never able to save ourselves

Full Spectrum

For Emmett, Breona, George, Tyre, and all the other murdered children

When the final baroque flyleaves close over this weary life
Imagine me in some better place beyond the veil

No elysian fields of lavender for me

Picture me running my fingers through saffron fields of wheat
Walking lush forests, tripping through verdant greenery
Or black velvety sands beneath my feet
Swimming in cool turquoise seas
Under an azure sky, tinged with hints of grey by day
An ultramarine mantle, by night,
with red and white starlight winking through

Opalescent hummingbirds
Coquettish birds-of-paradise dancing
Quetzals cavorting
Widowbirds wandering
Peacocks preening
A riotous cacophony among red roses,
Hibiscus, and chrysanthemum

Imagine me on some distant shore

Resting

Thinking

Waiting

Waiting for the wheels of time and love to align once more

Calling.

Pulling me back into the full spectrum that is life.

What Remains

What remains on life's road?
Youthful hours consumed
With trying to steer straight courses
Only to encounter surprise

At the end of every rainbow.
Seemingly amazed that things did
Or did not work out
Or took some unexpected tributary

What remains on life's road?
The clues left behind counsel us
Like fall leaves strewn on a mountain road
Fixed in place by dew or rain

Waiting for us to gather them
Call them our own
Embracing the lessons they've learned
About letting go

What remains on this road?
As we shed the old self
Blossoming into something new
Or perhaps to learn a new story

Finding new streets we've never trod
Or even thought to step upon. Always learning,
Always searching, manifesting
Onto page or canvas, or just an internal unseen shift

Love grows and expands, fills up our being.
Death, our second chair, our understudy
Patiently waits for us to join her in rest
As we anticipate her final embrace, fearless

The work of life mostly done
For the young to build upon or discard
By their own choice
No longer a worry for us

What remains on this road?
Time. Which always seems more precious
And better used when it is scarce

Until we come to its end

We remain open, receptive

To what is next…

The End (A Sonnet)

Once a small child, no real thoughts about death
Then I watched as it seized dear one's last breaths.
Too many gravesides for those I adored.
Tried thinking of ways to lighten this chore.

No satin, no trees cut burdening the earth
A sea reef may be the best final berth.
Cremation, a release into the sky,
Symbolically free of gravity's tie.

Pressed funeral beads might offer some flair.
Heat seems right for a child of the summer.
It's unimportant what you choose to do
With the husk. Make my exit work for you.

Knowing when you finally turn away
You have my blessing, my love's certainty.

Promise

We will soak in the sea
Wander the forest
Ride with wind blowing through our hair
Feed our minds with reading

Pour our hearts out in creativity
Raise voice and pen in praise and protest
Relishing all that we have put aside
Or neglected or ignored

I'll reconcile with that mirrored woman
Tell her and show her how much she is loved
Finally, nurturing each other
As we make our way home to the stars
Together

Scomparsa

Don't fret that I no longer love you
Nor that I have abandoned you

I am held in place by a body
That no longer does my bidding
My mind is still here
My Self is still here
My love is still here

I'm locked inside this mortal shell
This human guise
That slowly fails us all

The lessons I have come to teach you
Are almost completed
Some good
Some bad
Some painful
But all important
And yet, I have a few more to learn myself.

Your love for me is locked inside

My heart. I am not sad

As I take one more step

On the final leg of this journey home

How to Destroy the World

After Joanne Limburg

The world has a nasty habit…
Time after time we denigrate the survival of others
Pushing us all closer to extinction

So many ways we've sought to destroy
We've strafed, and bombed, and blitzed
Colonized, torpedoed, atomized, and pulverized

We have terrorized, plumbed, fracked, and stoned
Raped, burned, polluted, and defoliated

We've napalmed, savaged, ravaged, and pillaged
Exiled, executed, and when all else has failed
We have scorched the very earth itself

And yet, a remnant always remains
A bridge to a future, a seed of hope
A seed of peace
A seed of wisdom and sanity
Seeds of mother and father trees

Nature resists, reigning us back in

To review the lessons we reject

To reconsider

To begin again

To live

Fossicking

The clash of two seas birthing one destiny
Neither forgotten, both calling, pulling
Competing to call themselves home

Stranded between too many birthrights
None to claim as our own

Everywhere and nowhere can be called home
Ancestors set adrift.

Still searching for peace
Still searching for home

Predictive Crises

Staring out my bedroom window
With a telescopic view of the heavens
Seeking sustenance, succor, and singularity
In an immature world

Predictable crises
Force us into our bunkers
To hunker down until
The next crisis comes
As we know it will

Murals overdrawn
with painted on graffiti
Obscuring the messages by which we live our lives

Beliefs shrouded in temples mixed with political agendas
What do we call a God-Christ freed religious doctrine
and supplanted with human desires and babble?

Seeking to separate the wonders from the hideous

Admixing the scientific and spiritual

Why, we call it profit, of course.

A Litany of Fear and Loss (A Cento)

The art of losing isn't hard to master;
For those of us who cannot indulge
Memory of old tombs

Looking inward and outward
Remembering
love will vanish

Anger rots the oak and elm; roses are rare,
So it is better to speak
This illusion of some safety to be found

Our words will not be heard
Above the din and damn. The night is full
Of lost keys, the hour badly spent.

Standing upon the constant edges of decision
I am accused of tending to the past
Remembering faces, names, and dates

History
Seeking a now that can breed
The passing dreams of choice futures

Today I am a Black woman in America
Lines along my face
As if I sculpted it
Of buggers and bastards, no moon or stars
Veins collapse, opening like the
Lips of our understanding

Moving through our word countries
So many things seem filled with the intent

I will ask the angels of a creative god to lessen the blows
Because I love to live
Beyond the face of fear

The art of losing isn't hard to master;
We were never meant to survive.

Poems:

1. "One Art"—Elizabeth Bishop
2. "Apology for Apostasy"—Etheridge Knight

3. "A Litany for Survival"—Audre Lorde

4. "i am accused of tending to the past"—Lucille Clifton

5. "Recreation"—Audre Lorde

6. "blessing the boats"—Lucille Clifton

7. "The Lesson"—Maya Angelou

8. "Litany"—Mahogany L. Browne

The Fullest Life

The fullest life is lived in freedom.

Freedom to write about what needs to be said.
What needs to be asked,
And discussed and changed.

Freedom to drive
And not be pulled over
Because I *fit the profile*.

Freedom to walk a thoroughfare
Without seeming "outsider"
because I am too big, too dark,
too light, too smart, too dull, or
too proud of just being me.

Free of your judgments, your faulty assumptions.
Free of shade cast based on location,
Or class, or caste, or shade (of skin)
About who I am or can become.

Freedom to listen to my music
As loudly as I please in my own space
Without fear of being accosted or shot.

Freedom to sleep without helicopters
thumping overhead. Sirens blasting,
Or the pop-pop-pop of automatics.

Freedom to expect my children
And their children can live, exempted
From the perpetual weight of fear.

Is it too much to ask for this one life?

The liberty to live whole lives
Freely.

Echolalia

February twenty-fourth, a new poem begins.
It is the hind end of winter, the predawn of spring.
A day of dictators, bloodshed, and tears.
Franco, Chiang Kai-shek, the Reichstag in ruins.

Rumors of a new war between someone and someone else.
Threats of assassinations, mass extinction.
Millions huddled in shattered buildings. Wounds
Hastily wrapped, eyes pleading with us bystanders

Babies tagged, passed onto trains so someone
Can live beyond this day. Others tagged, sent to the front,
Lights to be forever dimmed. Never the same again.
Yet, we do not learn. We do not change.

Carnage becomes Cold War. The heavy lifting
of our hubris borne by the poor, the weak.
Nonetheless, we will keep on saying,
"Never Again!" over and over again

Happy Juneteenth

From Lincoln to Granger
To the enslaved, the imprisoned and the powerless
A two-year journey lost on the lips
of a nation still embattled, embittered

A not-so-new holiday to celebrate freedom
A single word, a blessing thwarted
We can choose our favorite version…

The delay of a government agent killed
along the way to deliver the good news. Or,
Withholding news to bring in a final
slave-driven cash crop for profit

Free, but not free
Not slave, not Freeman
Free-ish in a country we've never understood

Leaving broken families
Still broken. Broken tongues—Still Lost.

And broken spirits with new
status on paper but never in its country's heart.

Celebrating the end of human trafficking
Except it wasn't
Making a dangerous deal with the devil
For futures stuck in amber

A new life coupled with old complications
Complaints
Complicity
Conflagrations
Because someone must be the lower caste

Watching as this involuntary arch
Of freedom rings in a new era.
But by our own choosing
drag with us broken shards of centuries of hate.

Two years and two centuries later
Little changed.
Patrollers have traded their tattered rags for riot gear,
Whips for tasers and bullets.

Most lives still penned in by trauma,
unhelpfully and unhealthily treading water.

So,
dare I say.
Happy Juneteenth

Americans Won't Wear THAT Mask

Claiming insanity from the lockdown
Clad in craziness, we've known about for years/
Centuries, but have failed to voice

Anti-maskers, anti-vaxxers
Swastikas and KKK hoods shopping at Walmart
Gaping holes in masks
For breathing and eating

Attacking because racial tones are not quite right
Joggers murdered; cops called on birders
Assault weapons in Subway shops
Subway sandwiches mistaken for assault weapons

Who are we?
What have we become?
Or what have we always been?

Blame it on some new issues
Or ancient American archetype

Aberrations drifting outside
Our great American consciousness

Hate brought to this shore
Manufactured with our nation's birth
To separate, denigrate, and kill
It is our mandate, our heritage

The manifestation of destiny
Exercising God-given rights to be great
Standing upon the graves of the weak

Our behavior in this time, this crisis
Will not define America
We have already been defined

We are bullies with bullets. Terrorists
Dressed up in camouflage, and
Made-for-sound-bite power suits

(Believing) we are more powerful than nature
More important than any other being
Americans will not wear a mask to protect others
Although we will happily wear many others

Lingers

A true story

Laughing, walking home
From the rathskeller
Thinking we were some / place / safe
The smoke corrupts the crisp air
We smell it long before we see

The orange glow pouring over the hills of Troy
Flames leaping from a mammoth cross
Covered in expired meal tickets
Burning on the freshman lawn
With its requisite mob in tow

Complete with an octoroon dressed
As a Klan Imperial Dragon
Never one of us, never one of them
Now spotting us coming over the rise
Wishing he could disappear

The quintessential symbol of terror
Not in the deepest South
Where my parents lived in constant fear

But in the hills and mountains of the far north
Where much could have changed along the way
Except it never really does

Hope
Always lingers
Just beyond the next rise

Babylon

We learn the watchwords early.
Excel in school, don't get pregnant
Don't do drugs, don't go to jail
And, for God's sake, try not to get killed!

Knowing in the final analysis
Hate and suspicion will hunt us down.
Drawn to the scent of fear of being
discovered, outed, wanting, or lacking.

Born late and east of Eden.
Thinking we can outrun time. Fleeing
Dropout factories, redlined spaces,
Penitentiaries. All built to hold us in.

Is there a priest who can redress these wrongs?
Marrying past and present and humanity.
Bring meaning and purpose to existence
In a world set on making us wraiths.

Spawned in darkness. Struggling
to add substance to our invisibility,
To overcome inconsequentiality.

But, soon or late, we see there's little to gain
in this morass of animosity and treachery.
With hollow promises of brighter days.

Yet, we strain to run the gauntlet.
Spinning the wheel of life for all we're worth.

Searching for a way out of Babylon.

Once the Fog Has Lifted / Pandemic Pause

Time slips by
Mostly unnoticed
Gazing into the fog
Never seeing clearly

Rarely seeing the world as it is
Others as they are
Ourselves for who/what we've become
See into our true hearts—sometimes dark
Unable to read our own spirits correctly

We comfort ourselves
Saying we did not see it coming
Because we were busy, distracted

This story consoles us
Assuages our guilts
Soothes our conscience
But all is choice

A privilege and a choice
to walk through life
Unencumbered
Not seeing injustices and imbalances
Built into the foundations of our world

Not listening well enough
To separate the clamor of rhetoric,
From the ring of truth
Numbing ourselves to pain and fear
As it consumes our world
And slowly eats away at us

The pandemic has offered us respite
Downtime,
A do-over
A reset,
A time-out

When we rise from this fog
When we have buried our dead
When we have wiped dirt and tears from our eyes
Will we then be able to see
Or hear

Or feel fully alive

To review and to relearn
To consider
What binds us
To each other
To earth
Or what holds us back
Or keeps us apart

Will we have squandered
Our time in the fog?
Will our thoughts dissolve
Into the dust of old regrets?
Will we remain distracted
By oratory hyperbole
Or can we finally embrace
Each other

Embrace the lessons
Time and Nature offer
Or give them a pass
Again

What will be different
On the other side
of this mystifying fog
of obfuscation
Disease
Depression
Disorder

Can we learn
To be present
And act accordingly

What will change
What will be different in the After
Once the fog has lifted

You decide

Dual Citizenship

A fractured existence
inside freedom's equivocation
But never fully in its grace

Like acting white
But always still black
Underneath
Still other
Distinct
Divergent
Peculiar

Carefully
Drawing inside life's ledger's lines
Avoiding tipping the scales (of justice?)
Evading being outed

Walking inside a shadow landscape
An imperceptible bend in time
That has become our prison

Impossible to be made more equivalent

By your hand or boon

Nor by what we do, or have, or own

A vagabond on this lonely rock

Never being you

But neither fully ourselves.

Once Dipped: Emergence

Once dipped
Once sprinkled
Twice washed
In the blood of sacrifice
Of The Lamb and The People

Slipping into the darkness
Searching for a light from heaven
Showing the way to sweet escape
Riding a world in constant motion
That will not hold me

Softened by summers in red clay
Hardened by winters on concrete
Looking to ablate the past
And its chromatic barometer

Sipping poison, hoping it's the cure
For the soul-sickness of separateness
That occupies the terror zone
Of memories, of dreamings deferred

Stepping into a world
That only wants to take
Chthonic maturation continuing
Underneath, still becoming something
Unembraceable

Articulations

After "Song of Speaks-Fluently", from the Osage Tribe

To carry the misgivings of a long life—
Who wants that?
To face atrocities mostly in silence—
Who likes that?
To balance the burdens of racism,
of sexism, all manner of divisions—
Who enjoys that?

You have to carry life.
You have to face atrocities.
You have to balance the bruises.

Else, who will teach the next
generation? How will they know how to live?
And not die young?

Revelations from a Riot

We, the lesser children of your Divine
Confronting monumental systems
Designed to continually ensnare

Battling riot gear and bullets with voice and placards
While dogs and water cannons work
    Shoving us down the streets
    Making us dance for you like broken marionettes
    With few remaining strings

Your goal
Or so we thought
Was to disperse
Slake the thirst of your hatred
To shatter our spirits
Breaking bonds and bones

Your goal was never about dissipating crowds
    Never to protect or serve
    Anyone besides yourselves

You've tried to dissolve and devolve

To absolve yourselves of crimes against humanity

Sending angry dogs to chew us up

Fire hoses, water cannons to wash us

Down into your stinking sewers

To flush away like refuse,

Out to sea

To be reclaimed by your patchwork God

To lie with our ancestors on the ocean's floor

Perchance to drift across the seas

From whence we were stolen

Epode to Tedium (Are We Post-Pandemic Yet?)

What feeling
Akin to depression
Acquiescing to everything
And everyone
Allowing all thoughts into
Overtaxed minds

We see each other
Trying to look normal
Whatever normal is now

Malnourished spirits
Impoverished by endless waiting
Exhausted, hollowed out
Yet clinging to an appetite
For more

Trying to reach outside this colorless vacuum
Beyond the boundaryless of nowhere
Someplace other than this
Depot of ennui

To shake ourselves alive again

Awake

To be seen

And heard

Why I Can't Watch the News

Behind what you say there is always something else
The artful deceptions, sleight of hand,
Tricks of the camera, plastic smiles, bobbleheads,
An uncanny sameness that spins the world

What sounds good, plausible, made flimsy trash.
Carnage, death of civilians downgraded to collateral damage.
Upside-down economy for things we can
no longer afford and hold little value.
Pro-birthers, antiabortionists, absent social conscience.

Celebrating septuagenarians
grooming their stepdaughters. Producing
children to populate Mars. Or simply
Stating that God told them that this is the way.

Calling concentration camps relocation centers.
Stolen goods as displaced inventory
More collateral damage

Gone are days when Walter, Chet, and Dan

Sat dully behind desks showing us ourselves—sometimes ugly

To pretty boy talking heads spouting

Euphemistic twaddle tucked in agendas

As democracy, law, and justice burn,

Skewered, over flames stoked by hate and greed

Texas Educators Propose Describing Slavery as "Involuntary Relocation"[1]

1   "Texas Educators Propose Describing Slavery as 'Involuntary Relocation,'" NBCDFW, last updated July 1, 2022, https://www.nbcdfw.com/news /local/texas-news/texas-educators-propose-describing-slavery-as-involun- tary-relocation/3004871/.

Waiting

A virus has taught us to wait
And perhaps too much about ourselves
Waiting, patiently and impatiently

Waiting for people to perform
Services we probably never needed
At distances we struggle to keep

Waiting to perform our rituals,
The sacred and the holy
All of us now untouchable

Waiting to believe once again
We can be ourselves
Loving, anxious, fearful creatures

Accept that waiting is our new truth
Learning who we are and who are not
Waiting to be released
A return to a world of saneness
And a longed-for sameness

Each Other's Business

After Gwendolyn Brooks

We are each other's business
Each other's harvest
Each other's concern
Even when we do not wish to be

Synthetically typecast by colonizers
    Through the agency of color
        We rise from the same soil

Rising and falling together
    Our ebb and flow,
        Our oscillations,
          Our very vibrations,
Move in rhythmic consensus
    Fates forever entwined and sealed

Locked into communal history
    A common future
Indivisible
    But always divided

Seeking opportunities
    To find or return to a better place
        One worth bringing children into

Can we ever successfully lift this yoke?
    Can we move this millstone of hate
Up the mountain of redemption
Or must we,
    like Sisyphus,
        be bound to
Watching it roll
    Back down into the filth
Only to magnify our baser natures

And begin again
Over
And over

America, the Repugnant Republic
(A Golden Shovel)

America the Beautiful, 1911 version

Sprawled beneath the broad skies
Trying not to be at variance with the grain
Refusing to be deferential to imagined majesties
Working to keep our requisitions plain
Still trying to crack the rubric of this America
And what we want of thee
In a land with no Brotherhood
And bloodshed across every creek and sea

Entering this land with irons on our feet
As the beginning of a life of defeat and stress
Ever silenced by threat of being beat
Or turned loose into the wilderness
With natives who have also lost their America
Manifest destiny your fatal flaw
Ruled by insatiable beings, no self-control
Liberty denied by enacting convoluted law

Facing the world with nothing to be proved
We spent 400 years simmering in strife

Lording over those who should have been loved
Looking for a better world
And coming to, of all places, America
Suddenly dropped into the firepit to refine
Eventually learning there's only greed, no nobleness
No connection left to any divine

It's not for everyone, this American dream
Despite the so golden years
We've tarnished a reputation that used to gleam
And we are only left with bitter tears
Grieving a forever divided America
America, what do we want of thee?
The true spirit of Brotherhood
Or we should each travel back across the sea

Sobriquets

I often wonder to myself
When two white people find
Themselves in a room together
With the same last name
Do they think they might be related?

Like when I see Patricia and Danez
Smith at an event together.
They/We often joke about, fob it off.
For people of color it

Likely means
A singular historical source
Connecting us
By bills of sale
By plantation
By ship

My surname means
My forebearers were "property
of…" someone else

And probably their progeny as well.

Never to know our true names
Nor trace our line
to somewhere populated
By people we once resembled
More closely

Video Prevarication

Inspired by the video "Police Break up Easter Party in Pensacola Because of Coronavirus Rules"

Roll that viral clip again,
And see. The headline reads
Police Break up Easter Party in Pensacola
Because of Coronavirus rules

Look at the vid and see how we've been played.
Not 1 but 2 parties. One with white people
blurred out faces, to protect the innocent.
Moving through the streets like waves
Drinking, dumping garbage in the streets
Mask-less

Black-and-white film, with low resolution
Crackling radio chatter in the background
Orderly commands to move crowd and cars along
No threats, no raised voices
And no profanity

Suddenly, we switch to living color
Views up close and personal

With "colored" people in it.
It's a different party.

Wake up, roll it again, and learn
Troops with riot gear
    Confronting

    Running

    Chasing

    Grabbing

    Detaining

    Cuffing

    Threatening

    Cursing

    Abusing

    Arresting

    Manhandling

    Women thrown to the ground

    Guns pressed to the backs of their heads

You know the rest of the drill
    Arrested

    Charged

    Weapons

    Convicted felon

Tampering

Inciting

Resisting

Accelerated violence

Multiple people in custody

No witnesses

Police injured

Roll the tape and see 2 worlds

Not 1 but 2 parties

Not 1 but 2 standards of policing and protecting

Not 1 race but 2 races

Here's a thought. Maybe

POCs should invite more white people

    To block parties

    For safety's sake

You know, safety in numbers

In their numbers, not in ours

But we can't.

We don't live on the same block

Go to the same school

Shoot hoops at the same park

Swim in the same community pool

Worship at the same church

Trick-or-treat on the same porches

Shop at the same mall

Surf at the same beach

Run down the same streets

Two different Americas

Commingled but never united

Living in places where

We will never be safe[2]

---

2   Richard Tribou, "Sheriff Releases Video of Crowd Reaction During Arrest During Massive Central Florida Block Party," Orlando Sentinel, May 18, 2020, https://www.orlandosentinel.com/news/crime/os-ne-volusia-county -block-party-police-20200518-la6jquddgvbkflzawh2cfhbyrq-story.html.

Prey

Captured, catalogued, reclassified
Into bestial categories of prey

Extracted from our native lands and people
Language and indigeneity interred

Through Hell's Gates into wooden ossuaries
Packed like hand-picked fruit, into spaces

Most profitably, calculated and calibrated
Sweaty bodies, bound, in life and in death

Landing here with supplications and prayer
That our resting place would be kinder than our passage

Purchased, imprinted, and parceled out
Enslaved, persecuted, and tyrannized

In this never-ending nightmare
Shackles seen and unseen hinder our steps

As long as we remain your prey
Living testimonies to your shame

We walk the same road to perdition
Together

Birthing Dead Boys

My cheerless Icarus
Ghosted before amniotic fluid
Has dried on your downy, smooth back

Ghosted for being yourselves
Born to wars on foreign soil
For inner-city battles that can't be won

Because there is no *thing* to win,
No *thing* to ever claim as your own
Free of encumbrances, millstones

Looking for a way out of chaos
Distancing from hopelessness
Sweet streetwise seductions a step away

A quick hit, a fast buck, an easy lay
To push aside the pain that always lingers
Race, the final, unbreakable yoke

Forestalls your escape from gerrymandered
And redlined homes to the boundless sky,
Always just beyond your fingertips

Lured by the light, destined to fly too close
to the sun. Preordained by skin tone,
And the pernicious math of hate

Cheerlessly we wait for the world to change
Hopeful it might see you, my son,
Alive and bright
Living in the light

That the world might see you, my son,
For the first time

Ode to a Failed Coup

Inspired by January 6, 2021

No dilemma, only drama
With a side-helping of treason
A carry-in dish of insurrection

Pre-formatted comments
Telling those who do your bidding
You love them. But we know the dreadful truth

You love no one other than yourself
Rants carefully formulated
To foment, incite, and excite the horde

Transforming mobs into brainless beasts
Into their basest natures
Minions herded to the front lines

Dressed in camouflage in broad daylight
Strapped with AKs, zip ties dangling from pockets
While you hid downstream with other nabobs

Some still say your ranks were infiltrated
Nuancing your will and goals, but only
Because we're afraid to call evil by its name

Lest it consume us, and we become it
Or worse, find that we have always been so
You picked at flesh America cannot heal

But you alone are not the problem. Merely
A pawn, a symptom of our diseased hate
Allowed growth in our infected minds

Teasing away the veils, the hoods of ugly
Truths. No more hiding. We've always known.
The real terrorists are our neighbors, Real Americans.

No longer assigning blame to the "unlucky,"
The shit-hole countries or the third world nations
For America's slide from grace

America has no grace. Principles
Of isolation, avarice, cunning.
Greed and commerce, our key values.

Terror will never leave our shores again
It's now homegrown, and we are to blame.
Showing everyone, that this "great" country

This America, can and will destroy herself
And we can get it done all by ourselves
Because that is how America rolls

Well played, Mr. President
Well played

Smoking Gun

What will we say this time?

Should we point to his pedigree?
A Mayflower descendant, an alien student,
or Mexican descent, or Native stock,
Or no one in particular.

Shall we speculate about his friends?
There were too many, too few.
We shall say he got quiet or loud.
Shared his plan on Discord or with no one.

Should we assign blame to his teachers?
A lonely scholar, an abused athlete, the class clown
Hat worn backwards, who did graduate
With his class on time

Should we say it was his environment?
Maybe it because of his single mom, his abuela.
Why are there never any men in these stories?

Powerless. But power can be purchased.
To make them all pay
The last true Blue American,
Or is it Red?

Shall we place an assault rifle in his hands?
With only home and hatred boiling over.
We all become his target.

What shall we say next time?
To assuage our guilt and wash our hands.
What shall we say next time

About a boy and his gun.

Treadmill of Hate

Struggling to make headway
Quarrelsome voices fill the air
Propaganda over fact
Fabricated comfort over reality

Subliminal messages, sweep into
Unused corners of minds and hearts
Inherited biases, like water
Seeping into forgotten crannies

Moil and martyrs always reach the same
checkpoint of festered air,
Cool and disinterested.
Or interested and ineffectual.

So many miles logged,
But going nowhere
Like on a treadmill
Again, and again

We Rise

Like the sun that never truly rises nor falls
Labeled early as irrelevancies
An unfortunate consequence of our hue
Walking the winding boulevards
Of America's ossified heart

Too often deprived of succor, sustenance
We rise from the substrate of hate
From the cribs of isolation, untimely deaths
Anger and rage vandalizing our own hearts,
Undermining our personage, our histories

We rise to lay claim
To this America,
Our home.

Not Lost

We stand watch over lives taken.
Not lost. Kneading the language to make it
Easy on the ear, easy on the tongue.
Easier to swallow whole.

Invisible chains binding us together
Greed and vanity no longer concealed
Beneath the flawed cloak of justice

Is it chance or destiny that some lives are important
While others merely fodder for bullets
Pointless wars, victimization?

Lives not lost. Not carelessly misplaced.
Not dropped like a half-forgotten note from the back pocket
Of your favorite jeans on wash day.

Lives stolen from other human beings
Original sin, never far from our hearts
Conjuring up fratricide, genocide

Sequestered by careful consideration.
Early sell-by dates stamped in utero
Abominated, abridged lives condemned

Especially for those who do not look like…
Or talk like, or act like, or think like…
We do

Or for no other reason than those lives
Simply do not matter
To us

When Archeologists Speak

When archaeologists speak of signs
Of our passing, what will they say?

What will be left from hanging trees?
Will they find chips of fine pine trees
From burning homes and crosses
Soaked in blood and fear

Or bleached bones on plantation grounds
Never properly laid to rest
Or metal shards from patrollers' horses
At way stations meting out justice

Maybe they will find traces of laurels
And brooms we jumped thinking our lives were ours
Before our seed was scattered to the winds
By the capriciousness of whims and profit

Will they find butterfly skeletons?
Lying beside relics of our previous lives
Or the lives we had before that

Will we be resurrected, seen again,

As if for the first time?

Suddenly made visible by science

When archaeologists search history and find us

What will they have to say?

The Muses of Wartime

The muses do not work legislation
Bored to tears by filibustering procrastination
They do not ask us to bear arms or shoot at anyone
With anything other than words and thoughts

They do not ask us to march in parades
With streamers and confetti
But occasionally to stand on a stage
Utterly alone

They do not ask us to wear medals showing our worth
Shards of metal our children will later lose or pawn
Nor to wallow in mire
Slipping beneath barbed wires

They do not ask us to howl at the moon
Covered in grease paint
Clad in camouflage
Although we might if asked

They do not ask us to swim frozen lakes

Plant incendiary devices
Or place any limbs in harm's way
But sometimes to be humbled by critical words

The wars will come—and go—and come again
It is the human way.

Our craft asks us to hold and speak the truth
To not turn blind eyes to life or liberties or justice
But to shine our lights into every dark corner
And on all who suffer

The muses ask that we write
Stand witness and record
For those who have no voice

This is always the calling of our muses
Wartime or not

Because
There will always be war
And there will always be injustices
Somewhere

It is our way.

Invisible Tribes

Rarely seen, less often understood
The obscurely "other"
The dark elves, brown fairies, darker kin
With separated lives and nameless magics
Just beyond the caul around your heart

The sylph, the peri, the houri
Speaking in tongues
Worshipping at an alternative altar
Dancing the unconventional rhythm
Lives lived at obtuse angles
Almost the same, almost the same

In the shadowlands
Of surrogate status
Shifting your regard
Shaking your head in scorn
If you think it is us making waves
The nearly invisible tribe.

Wellness Check

For Rev. Patrick Warren Sr., Killeen, TX, 1-13-2021

Grappling with angels and demons
I am Jacob seeking a foothold
On the stepladder between heaven
and hell. Striving through this middle passage.
Caught between the twins of light and darkness

All voices clamoring for attention
Inside this tiny chamber
Unable to discern the dialog
Nonstop babbling, all screaming instructions
I long for silence, till I finally hear myself

Screaming, lending my voice to the chorus
Trying to be heard above the clamor
A red rose blooms from my shirt
The pandemonium ends, I stumble
From my ladder. My loved ones fading…

My only desolation
I had no time to say goodbye.

V

The Hum

Perpetually present. In the City, the hum,
We thought, came from the pigeons.
Or buildings, with wind whistling through them.
The press and pull against steel and glass.

A million shoes scuffing. The subways beneath,
clanking wheels, grinding steel on steel,
screeching brakes. The sound of the air
as they race off. Jets sonically booming.

Away from the City the hum persists.
The houses singing when all else seems quiet.
The furnace, the AC, water rushing
through pipes, the prattle of trees.

Rhythms learned or invented
Girls outside. The cadence of jump ropes
Slapping concrete in song. Somewhere else
someone slaps their child in a tempo of violence.

The freeway hum stirs up fears.

Conjures concerns of the noise willing me
Into drivers nearby, or the flashing guardrails.

The sea, calling my name since birth.
In her ebb and tide, the back-and-forth,
in her rocking and waving I hear
the siren song, "Come home."

Noise inside, set on "silent," waiting
for me to reach out and touch it. Stop it.
Or will it all seize up, like a hot engine
Driven into the icy deep.

And there she is again.
The deep.
Another servant to the sound…

Letting Go

For Kevin H.

First, one must free oneself of hubris
The arrogance of specialness and ambition
Comfortably ensconced in personality types like A, B, or C
Or perhaps another family of initials, ADHD, or OCD

We must also cut away dependence on stuff
As the measure of our worth
Those trinkets we feel the need or right to hold on to
With no rational thought or justifiable belief

But it is not simply the trimming of things
Or even the turning aside

The thorny bit comes in
Thinking we are the only ones, lost
And alone in this miserable state
But we are not

The issue is in learning to let go
For the loss of people and things will come
Whether we wish it or not

Learning to detach, as Nature intends.
Every year apples blush and fall to the earth
While flowers bloom—and die—and bloom again
And the cycle of life goes on

Acceptance is at the crux and crucible,
the heart of our suffering
It is in learning to share our all-too-human pain
To unshoulder the burden of insularity

To pour our brokenness into each other's cup
To reach for a hand of another in the dark
Then together we might find our way back to ourselves
And our way home.

Ode à Laranja (Ode to the Orange)

Deeply inhaling its transcendent aroma
Cupping it in our hands
Checking for the right temperature
And the proper resilience
When we squeeze, it pushes back
Just a little

Running our fingers lightly over the surface
Marveling at the texture
Turning it
Kneading it
Caressing it

Seeking the prime entry point
Making the first gentle incision with the thumb
Just enough to feel and hear the opening sigh

Continuing our practiced meditation
We separate inner from the outer
Putting aside the outer
We scrutinize the furry sphere

Plunging deeply into its fibrous core
Beginning the delicate art of partitioning
Still inspecting and lifting away the pulpy bits

Gingerly the tongue guides
Each morsel forward
We do not break it open immediately
But relish it
And fondle it
Rolling it gently and guardedly about the tongue
Feeling the salivary glands begin to constrict
In happy anticipation

Finally
We bite it

And the juicy
spiciness explodes

Trying not to dribble in ecstasy

Delighted with the adventure

Prepping for next allotment

We reach the end

And we are satiated

By this experience

Perhaps I'll try another tomorrow

I think I need to rest...

The Sea Goddess Calls

From oceans and streams
She calls me, longing
To the water's edge where joy and sadness linger
Creation and destruction

She chants in ancient rhythms my heart understands
The high-pitched tinkle of errant streams
The tenor of churning whitewater
The basso of the unsettled sea
Imploring me to remember
What is important

Heart pounding,
Keeping pace with the storm brewing inside
Briny tears scorching parched lips. She calls again.
"Is this a good day to come home?"

Salt water stirring within and without
Devoid of tears
No salt or water to lend to the living
I stand at the shoreline

Hunting, hoping for healing

From self-baptism, I rise one more time
Knowing I may die a thousand small deaths
I am resurrected and restored
Replenished at water's edge

Until that day
My answer becomes
Yes

The Dunes at Twilight

Drifting, skirting the shoreline
Water near freezing

Shifting sands, rolling knolls
Rock ridges and sea rockets

The ebb and flow, the breaking waves
Enduring heartbeat of the earth

Heron steps gingerly along the marsh
Scarlet tanager and Bluebird flash the wild lupines

Cattails clapping, offering benediction.
As twilight overtakes the paling light

The sea up-tempos to high tide
Calls us back

Back to the sea

Back to the earth

Back to peace

Back to home

Winter Is Coming #70

The colorful tableau of autumn laid bare
Changing, even as we breathe in its scent
Earth-bound creatures retreating
Promising to bring beauty back another day

Clouds shifting, shades of grey
Scarce interrupted by the sun's radiance

Honking and flapping, V-shape etching
Carving the path homeward
Laggards catching up with the old gaggle
Or forming a new one

Ocean's brightness dimmed
Reflecting the waning light from above

Senses drifting to dullness
Put away like summer clothes
Annualized forgetting of
The earth's adjustment

The light of heaven will return
Rekindling our inner light
Waking us from our winter rest
And all shall shine again

The Little Death

Worry is the little death
Chipping at the commonplace of our lives
Upsetting our balance.
It ridicules our joy
Upbraids our accomplishment
An indiscriminate axe cleaving good from bad
Repeatedly missing the mark

Worry is the little death
Incessantly causing us to stumble.
Pummeling us even when our abusers
Are no longer present

Worry is the little death
That shuts us off from
Love and affection
Stirs the niggling reservations
About being worthy
Banishes us from the light
And leaves us drifting into darkness.

Worry is the little death
That disconnects us, dissects us
Disengages us from community
Exiling us to a foreign, lonely land
In a private bubble of despair
Picking at the remnants we feel
Can never to be restored

Worry is the little death we choose repeatedly.
But we can choose a different path—just as often
Love, light, a call, or hand away

Chasing Joy

Feeling already overstuffed
The tedious and mostly bland hours
Teach our hearts
To hold on
To hold more

Tattered selvage
Dust covered
Tamped down
With all manner of weight,
bitterness

The mind perceives a noise in the distance
A stream or brook perhaps
Seemingly lost along its way
Determined to survive

The tangy aroma of wet leaves
Sing to us
To me, my spirit

Real or imagined
Signs and symptoms of life
Restored
Renewed
Life, an endless field

So this tired heart plods on
One beat following another
Chasing impending joy
That always seems
Just around the corner
Just out of reach

Becoming Ourselves

Every year
Every new thing we try
Pulls us closer to who we will become
And leaves the tiniest, sweet fragrance
Of who we were before
We never fade away
Instead, we learn
We cannot become something new or different
Unless we were something else before
Letting go of some things
And keeping the lessons from that time before

Single Socks in Absentia

How is it that solitary socks
Wander off on laundry day
No other day, with little regard to setting
At home or at the laundromat

Where do these socks wander off to?
I've searched washing machines and dryers
Looked into corners and trolled many a floor

Where do our souls wander off to?
When we separate into two or more parts
Perhaps nowhere. But perhaps everywhere.
I guess I choose the latter.

Perchance we rejoin our favorite hose
Patiently waiting for us to arrive
To keep our feet warm for eternity
As we travel the cosmos

Ode to Dawn

Before pride and person begin to slip inside.
Before the world stirs. I am here,
Alone, pure, elemental

Before pining and forgetting insert
Themselves, and old memories are threatened
By misremembering

Before the night's dreams are lost in wool
Beautiful poetic lines come and go
Unbidden, unmolested, uncollected

Before the timbers of doing and being
Begin to stack themselves like cords of wood

Before pain awakens the joints, birdsong seeps
Into this sanctuary of silence

The guardian of my heart stirs,
Calls me by my secret name to say

The dawn approaches

And she is beautiful ...

A Sonnet to Morning's Door

Evening fades to unsolicited sleep
Flowing into places of dark imaginings
Morning comes to pull me from the deep
Distancing mind from diaphanous thing

There are two doors through which I must gambol
Eyes unfocused, open reluctantly
Glazed windows to the soul, the preamble
Inner light shining inconsistently

The second gate bids me waken
The door to my room, alight from without
Reminds me life's not yet been forsaken
Reality starts to flesh itself out

(So much) love flows through and around that door
Bidding me rise, to meet the day once more

Hope is... (A Sonnet)

For Sandy

A desert traversed for those we treasure.
Prayers with no words breathed into the atmosphere.
Hearts beating out time's incessant measure.
In a tiresome world all too aware.

A brilliant sunrise, the tolling of bells.
A gentle kiss upon a fevered brow.
Every unspoken desire we've held close,
Desperate pleas to invisible gods.

A songbird rising from a broken nest,
With the resilience not to succumb or resign.
Steeling ourselves against the final rest.
Often the hardest thing to hold is hope.

Reminding us, we too are loved in this way.
Covered in hope's affectionate embrace.

Alchemy

We write, reveal the hidden parts.
Peel away layers of life and truth
Else the weight become unbearable

Transforming vitriol into softer tones
Pain into sonnets of hope
Make way for understanding

Weaving abuse into songs
Striving to calm the beast that lies within
Turn dross into gold,

Giving ourselves wide berth, a bit of mercy
As we contain, constrain, explain
And reimage grief and sorrow

We are the alchemists who decode the world
Asking others to see, to be, to act
Speaking the words they cannot say
Translating the unspeakable.

Fear of the Edge

Tired, on a no-name parking ramp
In a generic city
That is not home

Ever fearful of coming
Too close to the edge
The alluring edge

Not too far from
The icy, windy release
Silence, peace

One tiny step
Into the vacuum
Free fall

Other headlamps
Bobbing in the abyss
Pull me from my reverie
Breaking the spell

We are not alone

So,
Not today

Scriptor Poetica

The muses and I stir
Rising from dreamless sleep
On cloudless and moonless nights

They've let me rest, or so they say
Meaning that
They've let me put pain aside
Temporarily

Setting aside the twin blades
Death and decay
Love and loss
Untethered, wanting

A brief recess
Manumission
Opening my heart and mind
Preparing for the next battle
Marching headlong into warfare
Refreshed

Sentimental Trees

The wind stirs
The waving trees and I watch
As color worms its way through summer
Into Fall

We share our views.
Learning to let go,
Forsaking old dreams and fancies.

Yet in this moment time stands still
And we can choose to stop
To hold it.
To savor it.

Ode to An Underrated Food

Rarely the thing itself
Sometimes an adornment
A crispy succulent crust
Paired with the star of the show
Golden, juicy. Adding
Je ne sais quoi to umami
To make the perfect blend
Bravissimo, fat!

Gossamer Dreams

The end of sleep approaches fitfully
All opened roads closing; alternative lives spent
A few new lanes, some simply do-overs

Morning halo guards all we hold dear
People, places, things buoyed by knowing
Sustained by our heart's desire

Mind wrestling to gain a toehold. Clutching
At gossamer dreams without coming fully awake
Like trying to grasp the morning dew

Floating up toward the light,
Some visions will linger, some will leave
Breadcrumbs, some fading back into mist

The Fates, the stars, the mind, the spirit
Will each play a role. Illuminating
What can be harvested, consummated

And then, we will dream again

The True Cost

Coming now to reckon the cost of living
And the prices we've been willing to pay
Despite the '60s mantra, we can see that love
Like so many other things, was never truly free

Time is the only coin we truly own,
Albeit temporarily. It is the price
Of all things, with which we make our choices

We've one trip 'round the universe to get it right
Time is how we mark what is important
Too often we learn to spend it wisely
Too late

Catharsis

Loosening the past
Exposes a future
Putting away the childish
Leaves room adulting
Unpacking assumptions

Opens us to truth
When we do not grasp
We can receive
When we do not press
We may enter

When we do not turn our backs
We can face the light
When we sit in silence
We can hear
When we do not cleave

We can share
When we let go of what was
We can go forward

When we let go of darkness
We become the light

Elegy for Eve

After Ivan Marchuk

In this version the serpent dons his light
How like a gentle lover he croons

Beneath the pale moon, world still birthing.
Around this child of heaven

Newly risen. Still too young to know
Time will change everything.

Soaking in this new thing, life.
So little time before the disaster

of knowing comes. Before the angels come
Barring the door to a brighter world

Where apples fall to earth, un-poisoned, uncursed
And I, Eve, am still your beloved child

No Angels Came to Save Us

Afters Edith Vonnegut

I hope this note finds you safe...

No angels came to save us, and we unmade the world we knew and thought we loved.

The air is mostly dark. There is no orderly rhythm to the light or the climate. Chaos reigns. Yes, it rains and rains and rains. The acid rain soaks through everything, leaving an oily residue behind impossible to clean. Not that cleaning is a priority.

It is not too cold, I think. The air is poison to our lungs and burns our skin. So we wear suits and metal masks with information-laden visors whenever we need to go outdoors.

I started this note with angels. There are no angels here, but still people flock to religion, the two or three remaining. You can see the sacerdots in their white soutanes throughout the city, still proselytizing and prophesying, even as we row past them. A few still want to believe in something they cannot see. In something or someone in control, beyond the poor human design which has led us here.

On a positive note, we do sometimes see the moon at night. More rarely, the sun can be spotted through the clouds and fog and smoke. This gives us writers hope and so, we write these notes for future readers, to help you see and remember.

Work is okay, albeit mind-numbing. But us worker bees are not meant to think, only produce. Produce and make, to replace the work of the insects we no longer have around.

At my job, we crank out manufactured meals that look different from each other, but they all taste the same. Makes sense since they are made from synthetic proteins fabricated in the factory next door. The factory next to that makes the oxygen we breathe indoors.

No one has been able to make them smell different, though I guess that's tougher to do. Everything smells of stale and acrid sweat. The suits keep the perspiration inside for later dumping and recycling. No water wasted on bathing or cleaning.

We are pretty much confined to small districts, for working and living. There are so few of us its beginning to feel like interbreeding. There does still seem to be enough random DNA floating around that most babies are ok. But I worry about the next generation or two. If the air stays this wet, they will soon need to come with gills to breathe, even indoors. Who knows, maybe our skin will need to adapt as well.

Here, the travel is mostly on foot, by personal canoe or water-taxi when the creeks and sewers rise too high. The water is painted black from all the oil spills, fracking, and leaks. An irony for the times, all potable water must be purchased from the converted fuel (gasoline) stations. Of course, there is black market water...

I guess no one "in charge" believed the "Act Now or Swim Later" signs and advertisements, and here we all are, stranded. When the Big Change finally hit, all cars were abandoned, left to the elements. Closer to the big, shiny cities, there are water subways with expensive transfers To the Silver Magnet Train system.

I've got to go. My factory shift begins soon. I will write more later when I can find paper and a plastic bottle to leave my note inside.

Sincerely,

Citizen Writer # 1975312

Crafting Beyond the Half-Century Mark

Time and Age

Time and age come with a certain sense of freedom. Freedom of thought, more risk-taking, a different perspective gained from a long view of life, its attendant difficulties, and blessings. They grant most of us with a new level of grace, mercy, and forgiveness for ourselves and for others. There is a sense of urgency to getting our work done. But this is a far cry from the panic sensation we may have felt in our youth.

Arriving Late

We sometimes become overwhelmed or even despondent that we have "wasted" years and come to this newest gift of art or craft too late in life. Having lived a lot longer than I thought I would when I was a teenager, spanning more than one career, I am brought back to a lesson I heard many years ago but only recently absorbed. If a gift is present, there is no delay.

Gifts, destinies, blessings, whatever we wish to name these newfound talents and skills, can only arrive on time. Not too early, and not too late.

These talents, nor the results we seek, cannot be forced or

rushed. The right tools, circumstances, teachers, supporters will arrive on time.

What do we do while we wait?

In the meantime, what should we do? Grow your craft. Hone your skills. Keep growing and keep showing up.

As a mother and grandmother

I believe that who and what we make of our lives is some of the most important work we do. Yes, we do some of it for ourselves, but more importantly it is for others—our children, grandchildren, even for people we may never meet, who we influence. We give them legs to stand on, ideas and ideals to build upon.

Advice to a Crafter

I am a writer and an artist. Here is a bit more advice you can take, leave, use as you wish.

1. You will receive conflicting advice: write what you know, write what you don't know. Write what you feel.
2. Do not write only what you know. Go deeper, further, higher.
3. We tend to reside in one of two camps in life. We consider our lives either boring or brilliant, rich with material for our art. You decide.
4. You are not writing or painting only for yourself. You want to share or send your reader on a journey. What pain or joy can you bring to the surface that makes them nod along and speak?
   a. "Yeah, me too."
   b. "I am not alone. I am not the only one feeling this way."
   c. "I never thought of it that way." Or "I never thought of that at all!"
   d. Or feel compelled to drop you a note to say that how right/wrong you are
   e. Or compel them to craft something themselves.
5. Celebrate successes and triumphs, even tiny ones.

6. Examine, but do not dwell upon errors and missteps. Learn from them. Ask yourself, "What can I do differently the next time?"

7. There will be days you do not craft or think poorly of your craft. It's okay. No one is perfect or hits a home run every time.

8. Be gentle with yourself

9. Get trusted eyes and hearts to review the work, probably not your closest family members.

10. Join a group of peers. Somewhere everyone can teach, learn, and grow together. We often learn a great deal by preparing to "teach" others.

11. Also join a group of next-level craftspeople.

12. The adage that says if you are the smartest person in the group, then you need a better group is true to an extent. You need a group that not only serves your ego but keeps you humble, but never humiliated.

13. Be gentle with others. Give honest feedback, just as your own work deserves.

Keep Writing

Whether we feel the time before us is long or short, keep writing, keep painting, keep crafting, keep doing. All we have is truth—a truth someone else needs to hear or feel.

Earth Mother (An Ekphrastic)

After Pat McCade

Mother to all
Transforming stardust into life
With the amniotic fluid
That runs through my veins

I am the holy sky walker
Holy surface walker
Life-bearer
Life-bringer
Hope for the living
And respite for the dying

All truth and light
Firmly held within my locks
Commissioned to speak
Into all beings

Breathing sage and time
Bearing the candle of life
The sacred center
Until the other shore is reached

A temporary end

By celestial writ
I speak life and memory
Memorializing past lives
Molding futures

I am the holy walker
Mother to all
Guided by ancients
Wordsmith as shapeshifter

Speaker for the living
Orator for the dead
And for those who die too soon

And when this earth passes into nothingness
I too shall return to my home
The stars

J'Accuse (An Ekphrastic)

After Tylonn Sawyer, Pietà

In tangled sheets,
We make sweet, sweet love
Rattling the gates of heaven, creating

In tangled sheets,
We turned, labored, bled, screamed, breathed
And pushed our best out into the world

Behind tangled sheets and thin blue lines
You hide your face and everyday clothing
Marking and cursing my love as he grows

You punch, maim, bludgeon, and hogtie
Detain and search, taze, bruise and kick,
Arrest, handcuff, and finally kill him

Tangled in now-bloodied sheets
Hated, demeaned, battered, but unbroken
I stand before you in accusation

America, here is your wish come true

The husk of a life that could have been more
Dead, in an undeclared and senseless war
A victim of historical hate

Once, bright-eyed, fists clenched, swaddled at my breast
Measured prematurely for his death shroud
Folding him into the sheets of my love
Touching my child, my beloved
For the last time

Borderless and Boundless

After Lorenzo Herrera y Lozano

Borderless is the mind
Scouting the universe
Examining time
For all that life and destiny hold

No border separates
Mind and body
The mind knows what
The body needs
But is often aphasic
Or does it speak, and we forsake listening
The spirit ever-pursuing
Cohesion and balance

Boundless is the heart's search
For love
Stepping beyond borders
Of fabricated and factitious lines of separation
And slipping through categories like water

Our mind

Our bodies

Our spirits

Our hearts

Solicit love

Petition for peace

Long for sanctuary

Trusting that we will arrive at a safe harbor

Where there are no more borders

VII: Acknowledgments

Acknowledgments: The Work

Several poems in this book have been published in slightly different forms in the following publications:

Rigorous Magazine: "Love Recast in Fire"

Poetry is Life: "Translation"

LaLibretta.Online: "A Sweeter Song"

Fixed and Free Quarterly: "A Sweeter Song"

LaLibreta.Online: "Nothing More to Say"

I Ache in the Places I Used to Play: "Seventy, A Sonnet"

New York Public Library Zine: "A Blessing for my Future Self"

Hiroshima Day Anthology: "How to Destroy the World"

Fixed and Free Quarterly: "A Litany of Fear and Loss,
     a Cento"

Struggle for Freedom, Moonstone: "The Fullest Life"

Fixed and Free Quarterly: "Echolalia"

Ink Babies Magazine: "Americans Won't Wear THAT MASK"

Brownstone Poetry Anthology: "Lingers"

LaLibreta.Online: "Each Other's Business"

Rigorous Magazine: "America, The Repugnant Republic"

Fixed and Free Quarterly: "Treadmill of Hate"

Ink Babies Magazine: "We Rise"

Fixed and Free Quarterly: "Ode a Laranja"

"The Ocean Waves": "The Sea Goddess Calls"

Rigorous Magazine: "Single Socks in Absentia"

Fixed and Free Quarterly: "Ode to Dawn"

Hope Anthology: "Hope Is…"

Spirit and Place Anthology, Indiana Writer's Center: "No Angels Came to Save Us"

Mom Egg Review: "Crafting Beyond the Half Century Mark

Mom Egg Review: "Earth Mother"

LaLibreta.Online: "Borderless and Boundless"

Acknowledgments: The People

I want to thank everyone who has touched my life, offered support, provided space and those who continue to nudge me to be creative.

And special thanks to:
Peggy Robles-Alvarado
Mary Anne Em Radmacher
Sandy Yannone
Billy Brown
Kevin Higgins
Maria Nazos
Diana Ejaita